The Sea

by *JJI*

"and I am brick by brick"
-one summer D.B.

to my no longer so little brother.

Chapter 1

Life on the reef was always hectic. I remember when I was a minnow everyone used to weave in and out of the coral like it was their own personal jungle gym. no one worried about sharks so close to the land and the odd fishermen were after fish like tuna or marlin so I had nothing to worry about being a small angel fish. The only problem was my adventurous spirit. I felt I needed to see what lied beyond our coral reef. for an angel fish to venture far out to sea, beyond the safety of the coral even, was rare, but I felt I had to. The reef was colourful and calm, covered in fish minnow and mature alike. we all got along pretty well and we all had a lot of fun. The day I left the reef was a hard day for me, I would have had people following me had I said goodbye, but to my dismay Juli seen me leaving. I didn't notice her following me at first but then a day into my journey I seen a shimmering yellow spot among the seaweed below me. I pretended not to notice, thinking it might just be a chunk of garbage, but as I kept swimming so did the shimmering yellow among the weeds below.

I descended to the weeds squinting at the obvious fin protruding. "Who are you" I said cautiously not knowing who it could be. Juli disembarked from the seaweed in a shimmering green and yellow flourish. "I'm sorry, but you can't blame me for wondering why and where you were going" she muttered frightfully. I closed my eyes and sighed "Juli... why? you know it's dangerous away from the reef." She looked at me with a stern face and exclaimed "I could say the same to you! we have minnows at the reef and you're running on them?!" The expression she gave my face with that comment could not be any more sad. "I would have come back, I just wanted to see what was out here, do you know what that's like?" Juli calmed down and shook her fins. "Fang... just come back to the reef with me please, you said yourself it's dangerous out here."

She was right, I couldn't just leave. In a way I had seen this coming but I just had to keep going. I was already a day away from the reef and Juli new the way back. For the minnows sake she and I went back to the reef. Once the minnows were grown enough to take care of themselves I set off again. I told Juli I was leaving this time, she of course insisted I let her come along too. "You're to old to do this alone" she said "you won't survive a week."

*

As we set off into the depths of the open ocean I remember thinking it was what I always wanted, but deep down I had fear for our future. As time went by the farther we got from home and the sights were astounding. we past by a couple of blue whales who told us about a grotto we should see on our Journey. "plenty of clams there, wisest folks I ever met, but they can't see a thing" said one. "shame that is, you might be lucky enough for them to tell you the tale of the marlin Tank, but that's only if the divers have harvested their pearls" said the other.

So me and Juli followed the whales directions and made it to the grotto. the clams were huge and pushed themselves around by licking the ground beneath them. As Juli and I made are way up to the largest clam of the bunch we swam slowly and cautiously due to the large hammerhead sharks that infested the waters above. It was so different than the coral reef we had no Idea what was about to happen. there could be a shark around every corner for all we knew. Regardless of what we felt of fear we kept on swimming.

When we reached the giant clam we stopped and stared for a moment until Juli was the first to speak. "hello, can you speak?" she asked to the motionless giant clam. At first the clam gave no response but after about thirty seconds it opened and gave a deep muffled "yes, I can, at times" revealing a shimmering pearl within it. Juli and I both looked at one another in apprehension as the clam stuck its tongue out and let the pearl roll out to the ground beside it. "what brings you to this grotto, are you a diver in need of a pearl, I have no eyes I can't see you." the clam continued. "no, we're fish" Juli replied in a stutter looking to the sharks above. "relax Juli, if they were hungry they would be down here" I said trying to reassure myself as much as her. But alas It was not just her fear of the sharks there was also a large crate sinking toward us. "there is something falling toward us!" Juli shouted. "A trap for crabs" the great clam said as it licked up its pearl once more and gave a muffled "We'll talk later just get out of its way." Juli and I quickly moved to behind the clam now licking the ground and moving inch by inch. As the trap descended it hit a shark in the face throwing it into a rage attacking the crate

Chapter 2

Pieces of shattered wood sunk to the grotto floor. As the hammer head stopped thrashing about aimlessly it swam lower and began sweeping the floor with its head. Juli and I were hiding behind the giant clam as a nearby lobster was viciously ripped of the grotto by the shark and brought back up to the rest of the sharks with a loud crunching noise. Once the shark was back among its kind we slowly began to swim out from behind the clam. The remaining lobster blood still in the water surrounding us was enough to make any fish shiver, But Juli was especially disturbed.

The last of the wooden shards were slowly making their way down as the clam spat out its pearl again. "what was all that noise, is there something wrong" the clam spoke as a shard of wood lightly landed on top of him. Juli brushed the shard off with her tail fin and sighed "Just the strife of life." The clam gave a calm awe of understanding and sympathetically said "woe is we who care to be, for it's we who... now how did that saying go?"

Juli and I talked with the clam for hours as he told us all about how the grotto got rescued so many times by a school of marlin led by one fish in particular named Tank. The sharks were scared of them so much that when they were around they stuck to the waters surface so you wouldn't have known about it. They didn't start fishing for crabs around the grotto until after the marlin disappeared and the sharks arrived. The best defence against the sharks the clams had was the dolphins and they were rarely around.

"wow, I think the sea weed is greener back on the reef, lets go back now, I have seen enough for a lifetime." Juli sighed with shock at the end of our conversation with the clam. I looked at her with an understanding gaze but still said "I want to find out what happened to the marlin."

foolish I know but it was a passion of mine
to seek knowledge.
                            *

        So, I wanted to know where
Tank disappeared to, and Juli was hesitantly
helping me find out. My plan was to wait
until a dolphin came along and talk to them,
I thought maybe, just maybe, they would
know where to start looking. Luckily enough
it wasn't to long before a school of dolphins
scared off the sharks while passing by the
grotto. I managed to get a dolphins
attention, which for a fish my size was quite
a feet. I couldn't help feeling dwarfed by the
size of the dolphin, it wasn't as drastic as
the blue whales from earlier but still they are
much bigger then an angel fish.
        ``hey I'm fang`` I said
cautiously. ``Do you know what happened to
the marlin that used to be around here,`` I
sighed. The dolphin closed his eyes and

sighed with a light chuckle, ``yes I do`` the dolphin opened his eyes and smiled saying ``they migrated, should be back in a month or two.`` after I finished saying thank you for this new information I ask where they migrated to and he said to follow the west flowing water until it turned north and we would find them. So now Juli and I had a course to take, a new goal, save the grotto by going to get Tank.

*

Chapter 3

The way through the open sea following the current was a little exciting for us to say the least. Just as we were leaving the grotto we were escorted to the currant by Sammy the dolphin. It was a good thing too because the sharks were still nearby. Sammy was much larger than Juli and I and it was quite a treat to have his protection.

Once we were at the currant Sammy gave us one last farewell and swam back to the other dolphins. Caught in the currant we built some speed, Not knowing what could happen and wondering why it had to be the two of us to go and find Tank. I guess it was mostly my fault for wanting to know why.

We grew tiered of swimming down the currant so we went below it and relaxed in a small sunken ship. The ship was filled with algae and the copper trim that the deck had was rusted a green so it had been there a wial. Juli seemed to have accepted that we were still yet to be back on the reef and was now more socially involved in our journey. She wanted to explore the ship wreck more than I did so I just rested in the haul and let her explore for a while.

*

As I was looking for a place to rest an ell Slithered its way out of a moss covered box near the end of the ship. "who is there?" it whispered as it emerged. I approached cautiously and replyed "Fang, Im an angel fish, and who might you be?" The ell sighed and slid back into the box, "my names crystal"

Juli entered the haul and gave a light "Fang, you here?" I look back as Juli swam up to me and I cleared my throat "yes, I'm here and so is crystal the ell, she is in the box over there. Juli looked over to the box and whispered "Oh, OK" I started swimming back up to the deck, "we better get back on the currant before the tides change it.

*

Chapter 4

The currant took us miles
and still it never changed direction, So once
again we took a rest below the currant. The
water was polluted and we could barely see
through the cloudy water. A boat sailing
above was making a lot of noise and
seemed to be filtering the water below it, so
we swam up to it hoping for cleaner water in
our gills untill a nearby fish spoke to us.
"don't go up, there is an oil spill." he said
through the murky water. To say the least
we were frightened, both of us shivered as
the water got more and more polluted above
us. So we spoke with the fish, a small tuna,
still large compared to Juli and I. He took us
on a short cut to the northern currant the
dolphins had told us about. He said he
"knew the way because he always swam
there to avoid the nets from fishing boats."

once we were past the oil spill
our gills felt much better and we finally could

see the fish that helped us he had large fins
and guided us into the northern currant
which was stronger than the western currant
and more crowded.

We got as far as the mid Pacific
ocean before spotting a large group of
marlin. We swam up to them and asked one
if he had seen Tank and he told us he had
asking why we were looking for him. When
we said everything that had happened to the
grotto he opened his eyes wide in shock. "I'll
go back right away, just before he started to
swim away we shouted "wait!" so he looked
back saying "what?" we looked on with
apprehension, "are you Tank?" He smirked
and chuckled, "The one and only..." he
started back to the grotto, as we followed
him we warned him of the oil spill. So of
course we took the long way back.

*

We were half way back right
behind Tank when a shark swam right
through the currant nearly eating us both if

not for Tank Jabbing the shark in the face with his snout. So overall an exciting experience the only thing was when we got back to the grotto the sharks had doubled in number and the battle against them nearly had us killed. If it wasn't for the school of dolphins that swam to our aid we would have been eaten for sure.

Tank was wounded part way through and in the end he died so that grotto to this day is now defended only by the dolphins. No one lives forever, not even the greatest friends like Tank. Some times life throws sharks your way and there is no avoiding them.

Any way that is the story Sorry it couldn't be a happier tale. "Now go to sleep" The little fish yawned and replyed "ok grandpa Fang.. good night."

FIN

NOTES

NOTES

NOTES

www.ingramcontent.com/pod-product-compliance
Lightning Source LLC
Chambersburg PA
CBHW032033290526
45786CB00012B/2766